Cake

Selected poems

Cake

Selected poems

by Doreen Fitzgerald

The Ester Republic Press
Ester, Alaska

Cake

Published in Ester, Alaska
by The Ester Republic Press
P.O. Box 24, Ester AK 99725 U.S.A.
http://esterrepublic.com
info@esterrepublic.com

Printed in the United States of America
by Thomson-Shore, Inc.

"At the Back Door of the Crazy Loon Saloon & Movie House," "In the Garden on September 6," "June," "Up on Murphy Dome with Bob," "Vaya con Dios," "What You See," and "Wintering Over at Spinach Creek" originally published in *The Ester Republic*.

"Foragers" originally published in *Prairie Schooner*.

"Connections," "EATS," "Morning Tic," "Oh, That David," "Simplicity 1975," and "Sisters" originally published in *Seven Signs*.

Cover illustrations by Russell Mitchell, Inkworks
Design and production by Deirdre Helfferich, Ester Designworks
Edited by Carla and Deirdre Helfferich

ISBN 0-9749221-0-2

Dedication

For all of my children, whom I variously acquired, and whose good humor and enthusiasm for life has been such a boon over the years: Ben and Jenny Rogers; Chris, Pam, Pete, David, and Mike Toal; and Jon Emmett.

Acknowledgements

For his tolerance and good humor, I thank my husband, Robert Emmett; for their encouragement on this project: Renee Manfredi and Peter McRoy. I thank Carla Helfferich for her fine editorial eye, and Susan Walker Pyne, a friend who has talked with and listened to me since the fourth grade. Three teachers contributed especially to this poetry: Barbara Clysdale, who in high school opened windows on the written word; Lee Perron, who in college encouraged my fledgling poetic efforts; and Diane Wakoski, who mentored my master's thesis. Finally, this book would have been impossible without my reader, editor, and publisher, Deirdre Helfferich.

Contents

Easter Sunday, Lansing, Michigan, circa 1950. From left to right: the author's maternal grandmother, Mattie Lou Wheeler Allen; the author; and the author's mother, Velma Allen Fitzgerald.

What You See

A dog by the side of the road,
dead still,
becomes a furry carpet scrap,
the dime in a curbside crack,
a crumpled piece of foil—
bear in the woods, a tree,
flower in the meadow, rag,
rag in the gutter, rose—
in this flickering world,
where hope and fear
both govern the restless eye.

1944

Uncle Kenneth came home
with sandals and dragons,
Dad was laughing,
Mother cried.
The little robes with dragons
fit the children like old tears.

1947

In the undeveloped fields of Fairview Street,
we fought the second war,
crawling through the summer grass,
hiding in gnarled clumps of sumac,
surely poison, rising suddenly to shoot.

It wasn't tame, that war beyond the bungalows,
we died abundantly and well.
Animating weapons
with our tongues, we rose and fell,
or after someone's sneak attack,
hotly denying death,
we fought along the diplomatic front.

Sometimes we broke for lunch,
or called a truce, when some insistent mother
raised her voice.
Sometimes the war was called because of rain,
or couldn't start, held off by a discussion
of what's fair—who played the German last,
whose turn to be the Jap.
It was a game the grownups knew by heart,
as we would too.

Elementary Music

Grandma Grunt said a curious thing,
"Boys can whistle, but girls must sing."

Until we learned this fourth grade song,
I thought the difference only sat
between the legs and on the chest.
They added lips, the lungs, the throat,
beyond appearance of the body parts.
The song had parts, and we were told
to sing the part that fit our sex.

Our voices rose in unison, until the chorus
came around with its quaint permission
for boys to make a puckered kind
of whistling face; for girls,
a strict imperative to sing.
Our notes went "Tra-la-la-la-la,"
a dainty line of skips and smiles.

I'd never taken to the word must, preferred
can, and after school, defiantly did both parts.
Inside the school, I whistled to myself.
Soon I resolved to climb trees forever,
higher than my brother,
and wore skinned knees like a twin badge,
proving something I didn't know.

In the song, it's Grandma Grunt who cuts
the human voice in two neat halves.
Disgruntled, I wondered who she was,
quite certain there was no such rule
for singing in my grandma's house.

I couldn't see how it foreshadowed
things to come: dish soap and soft hands,
the absence of water stains on glass,
doors you must not open for yourself.
Complete instructions are enclosed,
preventing problems later on.
Problems, of course, are not without interest,
much like climbing down from trees.

Later, I always sang out loud, in my car,
avoiding the tremulous "Tra-la-la,"
as I drove across the U.S.A.
and the midcentury blues.
I warbled my way through the trouble I caused,
thinking, at least I made things happen,
and I still whistle whenever I want,
often in the dark.

Defining Matter

GENUINE LEATHER, the wallet said,
stamped in gold
between the coin purse
and the identification blank.

I was only seven,
and thought quite hard
about the creature who'd lost its hide
to cover my paltry sum.
Picturing a tiny pig,
small and valued for its skin,
I thought there ought to be a law,
against the slaughter of genuines.

Laws, I knew, keep people straight,
but when I learned to drive, I swerved
to miss a genuine in the road
and hit a tree instead.

Spain

Red as the blood of bulls,
dust rising
on the Mediterranean coast,
staccato heel on the bare floor,
framed by a mantle
of black lace,
horned rose pricking
the dry mouth
in the middle of Algebra II.

Down Home

Uncle Narm played the fiddle in his overalls,
until one night he walked to Swannanoa
on the tracks, and someone knocked him on the head,
taking his two dollars and ten cents,
leaving him for dead, but he didn't die.
He has a mule that smokes cigars.

Latt Mac lived on the side of a mountain
and he never looked when he drove up and down it.
He kept a rattlesnake, stuffed for fun
and a black snake alive for catching mice
around the place. He had a black bear
skinned on the wall and the grinding stones
from old mills. Aunt Annie worked at the new mill,
where they make blankets, not flour.

Great Uncle Robert tamed those bees
and built a pool for the finicky trout;
the water cooled the springhouse too.
When he moved to Nebo, he took the bees,
but not the trout;
it's lower in Nebo, real hot in the summer.
One summer, when Uncle Bob was dying,
we drove down home to say goodbye,
with a case of Vernor's Ginger Ale,
because that's what Uncle Bob liked,
and they don't have Vernor's in North Carolina.
Chew Mailpouch Tobacco, the barns say.

Aunt Margaret chewed, but Grandma took snuff,
until they gave her a hospital bed.
She'd never been to a place like that,
where they take all your clothes and your snuff.
They kept her alive for a long time,
before they decided to let her go.
Then someone gave her back her dress,
a plum-colored dress with a lace collar
and her best pin, and they stuffed her
so she wouldn't look shrunk.
They painted her face, and someone put
flowers in her hands, but she was still dead.

My Mattie never painted her face,
and she always asked what I wanted for lunch.
She ate all my egg white, gave me her yolk,
keeping the secret to herself.
The Wind in the Willows she read out loud,
while her egg money slept on a cupboard shelf,
where she kept and dried the orange peel,
liking the tang of its western smell.
She could peel the skin off an apple
into one long curl.

The Entrepreneur

Christopher Columbus Wheeler,
everyone called him C.C.,
handed out silver dollars
like he owned Mt. Mitchell,
but he just sold melons in Asheville,
when he was old.

In lumbering days, when land was cheap,
he traded his for a strong ox team,
muscle needed for hauling logs.
When Yancey County needed phones,
he planted poles and strung the wire
across the mountain, into the gap.

When folks paid up in hens and pigs
that winter there was lots of meat.
Then he bought a widow's cabbages,
because they were so green and fine,
the whole dang field,
and the table groaned all winter
under sauerkraut to eat.

Book-learning was great-grandma's bet,
but she sliced the cabbage and kept the store,
while he sold buggies and the first car
rolled off the assembly line.

He was a big man, standing in his tent
among the pyramids of fruit
that must be sold before it gets too soft.
He would reach in his pocket and look surprised
to find two silver dollars there,
then place them in our open hands.
He was prince of the market,
king of the Christmas orange.

The Man Fishes, the Woman Waits

The man, reduced to fishing for life,
magnified by fishing in the stream,
finishing his time with a bad heart,
goes often to the bank for trout.
The woman, keeper of a well-swept house,
goes too and waits there by the road,
so someone can be called, in case he dies,
to pull him out. She sits in the Pontiac,
piecing a quilt, patterned remainders
of her past—the curtains, nightgowns,
aprons, pants, and other quilts.

As he aims the cast toward a favorite pool,
back behind a tangle of trees,
mostly fallen cedar, two birch,
limbs swept down by the spring melt,
she keeps her stitches even and small,
matching triangle edges to squares,
alternating light and dark. His lure,
flashing, scatters light across the dash.

Leaving the car, she quietly shuts the door
and walks toward the bridge. Looking,
she says, to see if the berries are ripe,
looking to see if he's still there.
They did this every sunny day,
until she died, and he forgot to fish.

Influences

*It takes a long time
to sound like yourself*—Miles Davis

Grandmother speaks in the right hand,
as peelings curl from the ripe fruit,
and potatoes boil on top of the stove.
Across the table as grandpa talks,
an Appalachian cadence moves
while he tells us how the lightning split
an outcrop wide and rolled a giant boulder
down Black Mountain to the cove.

Mother, a strict impressionist,
corrects the posture of jig and harp,
while father's Irish swims in the lake
and he talks of radios and cars.
Standing alone in another room,
brother polishes the brass,
trying a trumpet on for size,
mastering the triple tongue.

Crouched in my room on the second floor,
I listen to the register,
trying to learn from the rising notes
the art of telling dream from lie,
fingering threads of light and sound,
colors of blood and heat and ice.
Potatoes, swelling in homely mounds,
balance the story's hanging weight.

Sisters

Two girls went riding in their father's car.
Red lights were flashing at the railroad crossing,
so the car stopped.

The girls were counting the cars of the train,
when a long girder from a loaded car,
the sixteenth car, pitched from the load
like a javelin thrown on the field,
piercing the car front to back, windshield to windshield,
taking the children's arms:
the right arm of Mary, the left arm of Margaret Ann.

As the stumps healed, they discovered
they could read a book, sitting side by side:
the left hand of Mary holding the book,
the right hand of Margaret, turning the page.

They were often seen together. I saw them once.
They were standing at the table,
opening up some presents with both hands.

Speed

Richard A. Ballentine, 1940-1961

What about steak, inch thick,
heaped with mushrooms
grown by Pennsylvanian elves?
I've got no time to heap my sirloin
with morels; soybeans fall into the grill
and the wild greens wilt
before I get back home.

And my accelerator—
man, I get behind the wheel,
I tell myself I will,
press that baby to the floor
and burn up the road.
Which road?
"I don't know, but I can't stop
until I get there."

Dick said that, right before
he forgot to stop
and stopped his head
on the steel of the other
automobile, and the priest
said, "You'll all go to hell
if you don't slow down,"
and some of us are burning still.

Dog Days

The languid heart is on the porch,
slowly swinging back and forth,
trying to beat the heat.
The brain is in a maple tree,
prehensile toes around a branch,
studying its wrinkled feet.

The heart sips ice-cold lemonade,
ignoring summer's grand parade,
but the dogged eye looks out to see
who's passing by on Passion Street,
admiring all the butts and toes,
and that's the way the summer goes.

Ready or Not

The poem she didn't write in 1958
sits in an all-night diner,
drying its wings.
They open and close,
open and close
to the sound of crockery and spoons.
The head moves slightly,
left to right,
its leafy camouflage, a book.
Rising and falling, the dappled eye
flirts with the nectar between the lines.

Under the table, thin legs twine
around each other, holding down
the emergent body's tensile form.
Flesh winks between the shoe and hem,
all of the white space
dressed in black,
part nun and part bohemian.
Cream spills over the pitcher's lip,
a whirlpool in the scalding cup.
Smoke mingles with the rising steam.
A lepidopterist steps in.

From the Far Side

I like to think I'll find you again,
when we grow old,
our circumstance faded
in books of dry photos,
raising no eyebrows on my street.
I'll give you tea, I'll have some too,
we'll talk. You'll tell me
how you went back to Montana
to chase wild horses.
I'll tell you
how I finally got over the habit
of crossing and uncrossing my legs.
We'll trace the lives of your children
in the lines of the carpet,
then we'll trace mine.
I expect to have so much to say,
after my hair turns blue.

Oh, That David

David R. Wilson, 1944-1968

When I talked to mother on the phone,
she mentioned that David was killed in the war,
and I said, David Who?
I'd not seen this particular David for twenty years.

Yes, I remember hearing he was chosen for the Point,
and another year, he found a wife.
I can't find his face; we talk of other things.

It doesn't come until the middle of the onion soup.
He floats by standing in a proud pose
struck for my first camera.

He is smiling summer in short white pants,
for he's finally allowed
to pull his wagon to our yard all by himself.

The Foragers

All spring we combed the roadside
for free food—the young
shoots of milkweed,
asparagus before it bolts,
the fiddlehead coiled like a green fist
thrust into the air.

Often there was no meat on the plate,
and flavor swam in an ocean of gravy
poured on biscuits,
as both of us whimpered, meat to cut.
Dandelions bit the tongue,
the berries fought back.

We once ate the flesh of a startled deer
thrown skyward by our moving car.
Knowing enough to let it cool,
we hung it first from an acorn tree,
but never thought of using hide
to make new coverings for warmth.

The bittersweet I found and bunched,
each orange berry in a sprung case,
was not edible at all. It hung that winter
on the whitewashed wall like a hand,
the small tendrils, stiff and curled,
remarking how it gripped the fence.

Sometimes we fished for a meal
through the ice, chipping our way in
like burglars, keeping still.
We sank the bait and jigged the lines,
luring the prey we couldn't see,
a fish that may or may not bite.

When the ice thickened and the car wore out,
because we could not eat the wall,
and the months of gathering by the road
are far too brief,
one of us must leave, I said,
and when he didn't move, I did.

Morning Tic

Balanced on the wire
between sleep and light,
the body reaches out,
right foot slowly
inching
to the right,
only to find the sheets
stretched tight and clean.

Composure, 1974

for Libby and Scott

So I talk too much, nervously twitching, going on asking impossible questions, asking my friends when I know they can't answer and it's not fair but I can't help it and say I'm alone, I mean whiskers and toenails, it's not taking care of itself. Tomorrow I'll go to the Elk's Club, or down to the Pub and be lonely together and come home later and probably take the grapefruit rinds out to the compost pile. On the way I'll meet this jay, not a terribly attractive bird, habit-wise. But it will be indelibly blue and will fly up across the back fence in a certain way, and I'll be lonely and happy, contradicting the magazines, and I'll be able to tell my friends, "a bluejay flashing in my yard!"

Linc and Bernie

I know a man so wild,
he throws his knife
across the room so hard
it sticks in the wall,
quivering like an arrow.
He keeps a big ax in the city,
for firewood, not people.
Only chopped up the chair,
forgetting there wasn't
a fireplace, only burned it
in the middle of the room.
He is my friend and doesn't
frighten me, although
I worry he might dislocate
his shoulder or his heart.
My other friend sits
on the radiator,
reading books of anarchy
to cans of tuna fish
and sometimes me.
I hope he finds
a more comfortable chair.

Simplicity 1975

There was once a woman who sewed
herself a husband with French seams,
a skin of chamois
and various woolly parts.
He kept her warm on winter nights
and sitting in the second chair
was easy company.
He didn't require much care,
occasional repair.
Blue eyes at first, she tired of those
and gave him crystal green.
He always smiled;
the embroidery was exquisite.
She got the idea from Jamie's rabbit.
"It's true, he doesn't work," she said,
"but then, he is so huggable
and eats so very little."

Projection

If, when you're in Tulsa, cradled on the edge
of 5 p.m., nursing a cold beer,
and the waitress leans on the Formica and smiles,
when I'm in Chicago, having gyros and wine,
and a voice from the table behind me
scatters the mind, it doesn't matter now.

If wavelengths in the underlight
can break the resolution
of a year and a thousand miles,
it doesn't matter yet;
you're not in Oklahoma, dear,
and I've already eaten at the Parthenon.

Connections

If you win her heart,
be good to Geraldine,
she knows a hit man
in Skokie. He lives
with his mother
on a townhouse block,
drinks Drambuie
on the rocks,
and always wears a hat
for the kill.
Geraldine's cousin,
once removed, he loves
her twice-removed and once
removed a quarterback
who left her in the lurch.
If you win her heart,
be good to Geraldine;
a hit man's waiting
for the phone to ring.

Eats

Somewhere between Sioux City and Joliet,
I can't decide
if I'm the trucker,
the truckstop, or the truck.
Sometimes I'm the waitress,
my name is Betty Lou,
and I love you because you go
to places I can't pronounce.
You love me
because I smile.
Sometimes,
I only wish to hit the road.

Liberation

Black as the night is long,
white hot lightning,
cool sweet jazz,
finding a corner in the back room,
climbing the spine.
Downbeat punctuates the glass,
a trumpet stares,
the sax replies, we shine.
The keyboard rises from the floor,
and all the doors fly open
at one time.

Teeth

Wanda keeps hers
on the mantle,
because they don't fit.
Grandmother's leer
from the glass.
Lou doesn't have any,
he works with his hands.

Looking for Dad

Driving north, a low sky holding rain,
red-tailed hawk careens
beneath an out-bound plane,
streaming from the runway at O'Hare.

Sprung from the radio into the car,
Maynard Ferguson's trumpet blares.
Music rises from a Monon church,
washing the face of an unlit bar.

My father drives with broken hands,
holding his credit between his teeth.
This Sunday jazz propels me north,
scanning the ditches for his song.

On the Perimeter

The farm wife's gladiolas fence
a garden tended for the table's sake—
gladiators defending color
against the tint of cattle and grain.

The earthy coliseum boasts
a host of strong-legged specimens,
standing up to summer heat,
green swords ordered on long stems.

Their ruffled blooms like vibrant flags,
they show themselves to passing cars
in colors he would never grow,
and she would never wear.

July

The cuckoo, the rain crow,
calls across the field,
the sky is heavy,
the barrel dry.
Flashing the stripe
on his fat tail,
a young skunk bluffs a truck.

Learning to Read

Reading everything since the first grade,
boxes of Wheaties, Cheerios, Tide,
the side of ketchup bottles, Robert Burns.
Finding letters of the alphabet on the side
of a Noxema jar, in the john on the can,
I think I need a new library card, but the phone rings.
Pornographic Nancy Drew
hidden under the bathroom towels,
Shakespeare as Literature, Sonnets of Ecology,
Freudian Grease in 20th Century Soap.

Dead at the age of 86, Thomas Hart Benton said,
"You've got to take the warts with the good stuff,"
as he painted the Klu Klux Klan
into the statehouse wall.
Sign on the wall of my apartment house:
No Deliveries Made To An Unlocked Box,
so I carry my key and use it daily,
hoping someone will steal my mail.
Stolen mail, and I'd feel like a solid citizen crying Thief!
Locked doors, taking the cure,
Norman, as in the hit song, Mailer.

Brother comes home to visit with nine avocados
stuffed into his case with his clean shirts
and classified papers: Missile, Missile Guidance,
Guidance System, one for each avocado.
The banjo turning red, white, and blue—
swimming pool red, trumpet blue.
Oh the brass, the brass of that early band,
sharp as the intent to dance
around the concrete kitchen, into the trees.

A poet sings on the attic stair,
gnawing a loaf of stale bread.
"Stop killing yourself the slow way," she says.
"No problem, kid," he says,
killing himself the slow way,
jazz, jazz, jazz.
Slicing it thin on Friday afternoon,
stoned on the idea of no idea for two whole days,
call the sax man and the druggist—
play it like it is.

The little red hen runs down the street—
the spiders are loose, and Nancy's tied.
The drummer murders the alphabet;
a thief is robbing the mailman blind.
Near the avocado kitchen sink,
the telephone rings off the hook,
as the trumpet courts the saxophone
and they run to sea in a vegetable boat.
When the cereal box gives up its prize,
Freud runs away with a greasy plate.
and Nancy fingers the loosened rope.

When the redbud blooms, we celebrate,
not going hog wild,
because we know it's the chickens
and the cows, as we listen to the wolves
and Taj Mahal on stereo long-play,
talking to each other under a full-blown moon.

Filler

MAPUTO, MOZAMBIQUE— Even the tallest man fell down, on January twenty-first, the tallest in the world he was, walking toward a normal lunch, slowly in his simple house.

Gabriel E. Monjane was eight point zero seven five feet high, but after all, after the fall, the coffin measured eight feet long.

What was he thinking on the way back down? What happened to the fraction of an inch?

A Gold Star Mother, Schooled

She doesn't see enough to churn
or bake the biscuits anymore,
but on the table, still she keeps
a honey dish of angled glass.
The table bears the muted scars
of boys who dodged their vegetables:
one who skidded to a stop
to battle every lesson plan
and one who loved to model planes
with little knives and pungent glue.

Across the plane of polished oak,
she spread a European map
and learned to follow, inch by inch,
the stain of footholds gained and lost.
The second map she bought would show
a spreading ocean, west to east,
where smoking islands dot the blue.

She even marked the rosy place
that holds the loosened bones of one,
but had to dream the healing grass
to fall and weep, not knowing
if the grass could grow.
The other, in the unmarked ocean moves.

Eight pillows anchor down her room,
a fringe of gold around the silk
that frames her red geography:
a litany of islands strewn
like pearls across a wooden chest;
Paris on a rosewood chair,
the Tower of London by her head,
Rome, the footboard of the bed—
index to the known and parceled world.

Vows

Cross my heart and hope to die,
stick a needle in my eye.

Crossing the heart with a certain x,
needle sworn to pierce the eye,
a finger singes the hide-bound breast.
The tongue ties into a double knot,
wrapping in better a box of worse,
only the index finger crossed:
I never really hoped to die.

The binding loosens over time,
a leveler of hills and words,
the wrong identity inscribed
around the finger of one hand.
Standing with the undone box,
I shuffle through a pack of lies,
one scorched into the wooden chest.
A lid shuts down on the wounded eye,
salt drops kissing the reddened tongue.

Sooner or later, the fingers itch,
and the index crooks toward the chest.
I'm lying now upon this bed,
where only a few mistakes were laid.
You too could lie among these ferns
with my learned finger
and chastised tongue,
both cured and still, I swear.

Jack + Judy

She was stuck on him like a three-cent stamp
on a postcard showing a roadside diner
shaped like a hat;
stuck like a stool on a chrome stem
waiting to swivel a customer,
or the naked thigh on a summer day
clinging to the vinyl seat.

He could read her like a two-bit cook
reads a scribbled order
jammed on a spike,
fluttering under the greasy fan;
like egg on a fork between the tines,
or a hot beef sandwich between the teeth.

Together, they're waiting on the night,
halfway between Peoria and Baton Rouge,
where the word OPEN, in red block letters,
hangs under the words, EAT HERE,
spelled out in perfect blue.

Real Estate

We scuttled like hermit crabs
from shell to shell,
each borrowed house a ready-made,
our flesh the only furnishing.
Often it was a tight fit,
backbone curved against the will,
a foot in Cinderella's shoe.

Some shells look like small boats
unsuitable for anything but drift—
"Si si, she wants a sail."

Can you hear my skin?
It bristles when the chalkboard
scrapes the beach.
Virginia Beach in 1969,
when your mother forgot to go to Mass
for three days running
and the beads went limp;
when the children buried themselves
to the neck, their little heads
on the white sand like lumps of sugar
in the bowl of time.

"You can't get here from there,"
they said, "the only bridge has fallen down."
London!Do it in the spring.
It was a town where all the doors
wore lions with gold rings
and we had to knock
before we reached for the brass knob.
It turned in our hands and slipped,
like jellyfish, greased at low tide.

Of course, we had other homes—
small pockets in library books,
a hole in the ax,
space between mothballs in the chest.
In the desert we lived in saguaro's arms
like birds. It was a way of life.
The spikes will tell us what we do not know:
the sound of midnight falling
on a rock; how many moonbeams
fit the ear; the ratio of sand to glass.
"C'est la vie," we declare, to find out
things like this,
after we've boiled the blue crabs,
eaten the best parts,
and dressed the berries in cream.
How sudden these facts.
We swallow the grit and hope for pearls,
shifting in a narrow room,
until we grow too large for the dead
and find another place to live.

Cincinnati Blue

In the asylum on the right side
of the brain, where we line up
the dead cats next to the little birds
they ate and decline the fur coat,
where we keep close count on our ammunition,
the ten best kisses, ill-gotten gains,
and lottery numbers that can't win maybe;
there, a lady of perpetual motion
walks toward the curb, pushing
her chrome cart with its tiny wheels,
wearing five sweaters at the same time,
all of them buttoned wrong.

On the bus to the asylum,
the smell of old sweat and wet wool
mingles with the odor of burnt tobacco,
Wild Irish Rose, and unhealed wounds,
under the fragrance of false scent
splashed on faces, neck, wrist,
in the frantic orchestration
of unrelieved hope, or the calm
despair of a bad shoe. When the picture
roils behind the eye and you listen
for a message from your radio teeth,
you might forget to breathe.

On the soft wall of the asylum,
a small flower begins to grow, weeping
its own leaves. A dog walks over
and claims the spot, a bird comes out
of its hiding place, a bird revealed
on a field of stark blue sky,
as if the wall was mental only mental
after all, somewhere between the two
sides of the brain, and anyone can climb it
anytime you remember to breathe
in deeply the dog, the bird,
the flower, and the exquisite faces
on the unrelenting bus.

Bouquets

When someone sends you flowers,
or brings them in, swings through the door
in a gust of March and aftershave,
they will be beautiful. They'll fade.

Press the memory and save the wires.
Someday, if doors don't open on a smile,
you'll have the wires, the pot, the holding clay.
in May the woods are laced with bloom.

Cake

They say you can't
have it
and eat it too,
but then,
while you're chewing,
it's all yours.

Birds

Here is a man with one sock,
a restless owl with a gold band.
The ankle glares above his shoe.

Here is a man on a long rope,
waving one foot, one hand,
he is not a swan.

A thin boy on an orange kite
is sniffing the wind,
his back to a dune.

Antic in the window frame,
they move across
my straightened room.

Children call across the lake,
echoing the loon,
the loon replies.

Change

Living on Richard Tuttle's couch
is not large.
A cactus wanders through the room
playing the Mexican dance
on a brass flute.
A vine grabs the window frame.
Living on Richard's couch
is not the street
with no place left to park.
Tuttle's rug is red,
his thumbs are green.
Unseen this week—his empty
cup by the hot air grate,
an unwashed plate,
swelling in the sink.
My directions to the lake,
like a one-way street,
left in my lost jeans.
Neighbors in this dream
knock on the open door
to borrow salt.

Blue Rondo after War

Playing delectable jazz guitar,
sweetened by the bass,
Bruce, with a serious face,
makes a musical joke.
Stroking the neck of a second beer,
my fingers smile at the serious ear,
and the music takes us where it goes—
we fly to Rio and conquer Rome.
It's a fifty-cent cover, Front Street bar,
with no one guarding the alley door,
so a man slips into the smoky air
to save us for the second set.

Guarding his face with a thin arm,
he hurls a stick across the room,
into the jungle on the wall,
the one that only he can see.
When he overturns an empty chair
and crouches there as the music plays,
he aims his fingers past the stage,
and bullets fly from his empty hand,
pinning a deadly shadow down.

When he rights the chair and spots
loose change, he sits to bum a beer from me
and tell me of his only song,
the only one that he can hear.

The song he knows goes seventeen,
seventeen in one day, called back
like notes on the amazing player piano—
seventeen shadows, seventeen years,
seventeen faces in the snow.
White knuckles on the glass
next to the serious coin,
telling us who we trust—
the vet for his count,
Bruce for the beautiful tune.

The City of Angels Accommodates Simplicity

Among the others in the alley of packed red dirt,
a tall man, bony and dark,
lives in a cardboard coffin.
It is perfectly shaped to his frame,
the corrugated boxes taped,
as if the nails ran out.
The flap at the head is folded back,
like a visored helmet after war,
the knight relaxed.
It isn't raining and he isn't dead.

The unpaved alley holds five properties;
there are no taxes on the lots,
the lot lines shift.
By virtue of possession,
a family of four is holding title
to a slumped car; there is no key.
Dust has settled on a white appliance crate,
the home of Miss Agnes.
She has pretensions and a blanket of green wool
and wears them when she goes downtown.

A man in soft white shoes and clean pants
hands out leaflets from door to door:
religion, soup, prevention.
The man in the coffin raises his arm,
takes the literature, brings it in.
He hasn't any room for books,
his room arranged to hold the body heat.
You just can't live like this where I come from.
It gets too cold. We have so many books.

Last Rites for Dad at Summer's End

It was a hot day.
Graphite grease leaked onto my suit
from the window crank in the long car.
Everything stuck to us, but Dad.
He'd up and left the weather behind.

It was one of those hot fall days,
when you want to be out
on the lake, driving his boat
straight into the wind,
cross-wave, waving at other boats.

It was so hot,
I wouldn't want to be a grave digger
out in the sun,
making a hole to hide the skin
of somebody's father about to melt.

A real scorcher,
the kind of day you need to ask
to borrow his car and go for a drive,
crank the windows down
and the music up.

It was humid, too.
The air shimmered in waves.
Even the flowers could hardly breathe.
The hair uncurled;
the tears burst into flame.

The Boat Builder

A landlocked Viking in the Middle West,
driving back and forth across the plain,
he held no sword, no shield to guard his chest;
his only sea, the waves of wind and rain.

He drove, he learned the stars, and cursed the storm,
enchanted by his one intemperate dream:
to plan the hull, the angles of the form,
then plane the wood and shape the ribs with steam.

John wanted, when he died, to slowly sail
into the sunset all aflame; instead,
he went by car. His bones, now they must rail
until new oceans claim his inland bed.

His legacy was simple and unplanned,
a song of open water and the hand.

Food Groups

No matter how you flesh the story out,
the bones say life eats life.
There is a ham hock living
in my right foot,
a moose haunch walking in my other shoe.
Tofu is no exception, everything feeds.
A tree climbs onto the backs of the dead
for a better view.
The bean field kills the tree,
bread kills the wolf.
Some cows live on in service
to strong bones; the grass, to cows.
The pasture, like a picnic spread
calls out the bug, the mouse, a hawk.
Potatoes died to feed the blight;
one stalk grows tall
expending something else.
A simple caution gripped within the seed,
loose on the breath—
be careful what you eat today,
consider what you feed the earth.

Handyman Special

On the eighth day, we blundered out
among the tall, insistent weeds
to wander back and forth
beneath the mute and moving stars.

Tossed by the weather, dreaming house,
we looked, in our persistent need,
at the movable hand. The short
opposable thumb might take us far.

We made some tools to find and rout
both animal and enemy—
instant unrepeatable war
on the heels of a four-wheeled cart.

One day perhaps we'll look about
at manufactured speed and seed
and yet another ruined shore,
stick out that thumb, and thus depart.

What's New?

Over the heartland, a mongrel dog
is driving a pick-up around the block,
a red bandana around his neck.
He has learned this trick from an ordinary man.

Nearby, on an even plain, a calloused Scandinavian,
pagoda planted in the brain,
has raised one seven stories high,
inviting wind-swept people to look out.

A woman of substance, farther north,
has snipped a thread on the final knot
of a Gainsborough painting reproduced
in five thousand crosses of measured silk.

Another, on her hands and knees,
disturbs the earth to set the stage
for cosmos blooming on a hill, arranged
within a neat but ragged ring of broken schist.

Across the Mason-Dixon line, a house of bottles
once took shape, the heavy bottoms facing out
and plainly set in concrete
so each circle snares the light.

These givens, like old bathtubs set
to keep a virgin in the yard, and wagon wheels
to get the mail, get used for making something,
making something of the will.

Titanic Lesson

Chance floats on the water, hidden and cold,
waiting to show us how the sea
can swallow assumption in one gulp;

how space in a lifeboat starts to shrink
after the warning whistle blows;

how the music skips when it hits the water,
and a wallet gurgles on the downward drift;

how calamity beckons as we skirt the edges,
sniffing for underwear and jewels;

how flatware on the ocean floor
forgets the order of the knife and fork;

how long it takes to find a spoon;

how soon the bones of contention rise
over rights to salvage and exhibition;

how grave goods always come up for grabs,
and it's sometimes lucky to miss the boat.

The Cutting Room

We wait by the sea as a stranded urchin
waits for another tide.
The split moon is pulling the sea
back and forth, forward and back
like a black piano on wooden wheels.
We walked all night to reach this place,
the rocks as big as moons.
They were never round,
but the falling sea is wearing them down,
grinding them up and spitting them out,
like a necktie thrown from the seventh floor,
through the open window to the street below.

Sister Mole

Under the breathing carpet,
beneath the earthen floor,
a small and sightless neighbor
is opening a door.

She concentrates upon the smell
of beetle's acid track,
the notes of snake's brief lullaby,
the pale grub's ghostly act.

Beside a driven tree root,
between the frost-heaved stones,
she penetrates the darkness
among the fallen bones.

This subterranean mistress
seeks not a human breath.
She's feeding on the underside,
an intimate of death.

Solace

Annie's gone, my daughter said,
and it was so,
and there was nothing else to do
but choose the flowers
that she would never see—
daisies from a sunlit hill,
iris for the spring.

She's buried in an infant's field,
and far away, with no one near
to bring the flowers.
I think of her as in one star,
and gave a star her name.
It's Annie's star,
the stars are her bouquet.

Mother Marries at Seventy-Three

They enter the church through separate doors,
each trailing a familiar past,
like old shoes tied to a wedding car.

Thad at the altar, creased in a suit,
seems solid and close, like a sweaty palm;
mother, a blossom in peach chiffon.

He's not my father, I can't say dad;
his daughter watches, her mother's gone.
Our brothers stiffen their formal arms.

Five separate children of middle age
our wagons circled round different fires,
have fingered this loose change of heart.

Their modest holdings rearranged,
mother forgets where she left her key;
the groom remembers to crack a joke.

Both versed in the loving that cannot stop
the failing body's downward slide,
they already know how the hands must part.

The pews all rustle as we crane our necks
to see the promise that they make,
as if their future is our own.

A Woman Needs a Man Like a Fish Needs a Bike

A bicycle, that is,
one she can peddle with both fins,
the ones that center her scaled form,
which he likes, of course,
in his own crude way,
with his chain-linked feelings
and geared-down tongue.
You can move water with a turning wheel,
once you get the balance right.

Planning Ahead

My husband has named the goods for his grave,
the stuff he wants for the long haul.
We were having coffee, the subject came up.

Spinners, an artificial bait,
rainbow scale, number 1 aglia long by Mepps;
in the water it looks like a small fish
a bigger fish will bite.
A Super Duper, brass and red,
(number 501 or 503), which looks
like a wounded minnow for the same reason—
the fish: they way they take the hook
and rise; the way they give themselves up.
Catch and release, he says.
A fine idea, though I usually ask
for some to cook, because my hands
are linked to the stove.

He remembers the numbers of many lures;
the date of our marriage escapes his mind,
although he studies the American past,
and we did it there, in the yard,
where Stoney made the barbecue
and vows were almost an afterthought,
a promise to do the best we can.

Now I promise a spinning rod,
only the best for eternity,
reinforced with graphite, and the reel,
a Mitchell 300, made with real metal—
cast farther, won't break.

Put some dog bones in. Not the bones
of Mariah, his old dog,
who feeds the blue delphiniums
by our northern house.
He wants some bones for the working dogs,
a treat in his pocket when he arrives,
before he hitches up the sled.
He's certain their trail will be the same.
Why else would he turn, as a dead dog leaves,
to wipe the salt from his damp beard?
A grown man weeps for few things.

When the bike won't fit in the travel case,
he says shirts: Shit Happens, Live to Ride,
flags of the all-American scoot.
He has not named her, the inflatable doll,
a Bimbo he can take along.
Maybe he knows his other goods
will attract some dame,
one who will follow the flash of the lure,
or the slick odor of motor oil
and the scent of dog hair wet with rain.

Maybe he knows, if I get there first,
I'll stand on the trail in my flannel gown,
talking with the dogs, holding the pan,
waiting for some fish to fry.

Wintering Over at Spinach Creek

A tiny beast, the vole, goes about
this business of life so low to the ground,
etching a delicate trail in the snow.
My own thick boots, the lugs I wear for traction
on the steep slope, leave a different mark.

The dahlias, frozen in their summer bed,
their bulbs undug, will never bloom again.
Sacrificed by my neglect,
they bloom as separate humps of snow.
Food for the vole, perhaps, on February third.

Up in the house, in unison,
the green plants lean toward the pale sun
already low above the facing dome.
My own ear strains toward the first faint sound
of water moving under the earthbound snow.

The vole just goes where he always goes,
burrowing,
burrowing through a frozen maze,
using to the best effect
this clean and muffled arctic world.

Cornered in Town on the Brink of Spring

The stalled mind gropes like a wrinkled sail,
fumbling for another lift.
Where hot spots open the ocean floor,
tube worms dance on the perk and steam.

When a slit appears in the concrete walk,
flashing a strip of packed earth,
the shifting tap root sinks and holds
its green intention to the cracked light.

As the a whale drives up from the underworld,
nosing toward the mottled sun;
one corked bud on a milky stem
carries its spume of ripened seed.

June

Solstice runs toward us,
her feet and shoulders bare,
the smoke of wildfire tangled
in her golden hair.

She runs a steady circle,
I bend and crawl and lean,
making up the garden,
holding close the green.

Up on Murphy Dome with Bob

Blueberries, warm in the hand,
deep blue orbs of sunshine
in the palm. In the mouth
the juices flare, staining the lips
the ruby color of love.

In the Garden on September 6

I admire the bumblebee's
approach to certain doom,
as the earth cools,
and the nights grow long.
He's on Veronica still,
nestled among her blue spires,
nuzzling the last blooms
as she goes to seed.
Tomorrow morning's fog,
a shroud for both,
but even so,
the nectar is still sweet.

In My Cousin's Garage

Michigan is outside, the window brushed
with snow. Inside, my cousin and his wife
asleep, and my daughter sleeps, listening
in her dream for children's trouble
and discontent. Her children dream of sleds
and angels in the snow they made last night.

We have come to bury mother, and I still smoke.
Here's another hole in my black coat.
She sent me articles on how to stop.
There's a hole in Balcom Cemetery too,
where we buried father and all the rest.
After mother there's no more room.

When I die, I want to be burned—my bones,
not my soul. I want finally to blend in.
What is this trouble and discontent?
Who are these angels in the snow?
Would Dad take all his smokes outside the house?
Leave well enough alone, she often said.

I pruned the woods and poked the coals
and raked the muck. Mother, your mouton coat
in the car on a winter night was a nest,
your voice and father's blending in the air.
When you taught us to fly, you never said
we shouldn't land so far from home.

Alone among my cousin's tools and cars,
I listen to the door I slammed at twelve,
after I hurled the dishrag on the floor.
Now morning breaks across the dormant field,
and blackbird rustles in the apple tree.
I'd fly, but once again, I'm all undone.

Bagdad Cafe

When the breadbox overflows with crumbs
and you can't go out because of rain,
a friend may bring you things of the world:
a chinese taco, feathers from arctic birds—

or in dead winter, a southern trip
paid for by a senile aunt
who rides stretched out on the back seat,
shouting "Chop Suey" and "Grand Slam."
If she hadn't wandered off the course
on the seventh hole, she wouldn't be here now;
if only she didn't bite—

or how they caught live birds
with their bare hands;
reached through the fence for a warm meal
in a war we were born too late to catch,
then came back home and taught us Crazy Eights—

how we ride out on Route 66,
like dolls of all nations armed with film
to capture the buzz on the cracked wall
of the Bagdad Cafe—
how we pray in the All-Night Church of Elvis,
somewhere near Seattle,
and women of middle age
sit around a table making earrings
that jiggle with every move—

how the chapel points toward heaven,
good cards and hot food,
and we are moving now—
toward the scent of new bread
and the voice of a snowy owl
on an invisible branch,
toward a hand that holds
the ace of hearts and hearts are trump,
toward the place
where Bagdad's always on the map.

At the Back Door of the Crazy Loon Saloon & Movie House

My basket fills and empties like a migrant picker's sack—
someone waiting to weigh the take.
Darlin, sez Jack, put the basket down—
remember to look up.

The moon gets full on Christmas Eve,
and once, not very long ago,
I saw it so, it made the dark time gleam,
a steady eye that held my gaze
and lit the crisp December snow.
I only looked because of Jack,
who didn't want to hear me whine,
and told me then at closing time
that pleasure's in the point of view.
You can't get to the moon from here,
unless you look into the sky.
You've got to parse the stars a bit
to hear their music ring.
Aurora dances anyway and doesn't care
who sees her sway and sweep
across the smooth celestial floor.
I'm pretty sure that as she moves
she isn't looking at her feet.

There is a basket full of things
it doesn't pay to stop and count—
the sound of snow geese on the wing,
the way Aurora moves the night,
a parcel like the Christmas Moon.

The Scribe on Sheep Creek Road

Those black trees lining the ridge,
a forest of pencils aimed at the sky.
They write the rain, point out the names
we give the stars: hunter, virgin,
lion, bear—story pulsing in the dark.
As morning breaks above the hill,
and the sky listens like a blank page,
she scrawls a letter to the missing ones
in the margin of the day.

South Pacific

When I live in Fiji I walk down the trail,
whistling a song I can barely recall,
but it grows stronger with every step,
like an Outback songline moving the feet.
My feet are bare.

When I wear my hair long,
it floats on the sea,
and body remembers its first home.
I can part the water like a keen shark
or a well-planned boat.

On the beach, the ocean beads on the skin,
as I practice braiding the salted hair,
learning the way of native plants
from someone who also wants to tell
how seabirds brought them on the wind.

In the afternoon, I practice some knots,
one against evil, one for love. For this
you must make your own rope.
On the boat, the ropes are neatly coiled,
and some knots slip when you need to let go.

I carved my boat and laced the sail
to navigate with sticks and shells
the open space between our island homes.
Our landfalls, born of coral and fire,
rise and fall in the ocean swell.

At evening, when the sun sails off,
blood and rubies in its wake,
heat rises and the moon swims back.
The ocean intimate with both,
glorifies their coupled light.

Night knows how the southern sea
has a different angle on the stars.

Vaya con Dios

The body leaving
turns and winks and whispers
Adios, my friend,
then like an old friend
sits back down
to listen to the might have been
and once upon a time.

The body leaves
in fits and starts, in temperament
a cheap used car
desperate for some engine part,
transmission work,
and four new tires.

The spirit leaving
simply floats away,
beguiling us
to hunker down and pray.

Autumn Sonnet for Susan

When summer folds her arms and walks away,
and winter, turning, nods and blinks an eye,
the trees begin to rattle as they sway,
contending they were only passing by.

When winter snares the memory of birth
and snarls the shadow in a branching tree,
the wind spreads out its fingers on the earth
to comb the hill and set the tangle free.

We stand between these seasons like a page,
sometimes looking forward, sometimes back.
You mark the passage of an early rage,
I fold the corner on a dream gone slack.

Like dahlias flaming up before the frost,
let's heat the fading landscape as we cross.

About the Author

Doreen Fitzgerald was born in Lansing, Michigan, in 1940. She lived her youth and young adulthood in the midwest (Michigan, Illinois, Indiana). After graduating from Portage High School in Michigan, she attended Kalamazoo College, married, and had two children, Ben and Jenny Rogers. She later completed her undergraduate work at Purdue University, where poetry came to the forefront of her interests. While at Purdue, she gained five stepchildren (MIke, David, Pete, Pam, and Chris Toal).

In high school and after college, Doreen's writing efforts were concentrated in journalism. In the late 1970s she worked at a small Indiana newspaper and later as news editor for the weekly *Antrim County News* in Bellaire, Michigan. After graduate study in journalism, in 1980 she went to Fairbanks, Alaska, to see what it was like. She found out, found Bob Emmett, gained a stepson, Jon, and continued to earn her living as a writer and editor. During the winters of 1991–92 and '92–93, she attended Michigan State University, where she earned a master's degree in English. Today she works as a writer for the University of Alaska Fairbanks School of Natural Resources and Agricultural Sciences.

This is her first book.